THOMOND
RESOURCE CENTRE

Plassey, Limerick

Telephone (061) 334488

Competitive Sports Series

NETBALL

Sue Campbell

B T Batsford Limited
London

Typeset by Tek-Art Ltd, Kent
and printed in Great Britain
by Anchor Brendon Ltd
Tiptree, Essex
for the publishers
B T Batsford Limited
4 Fitzhardinge Street
London W1H 0AH

British Library Cataloguing in Publication Data

Campbell, Sue
    Netball.– (Competitive sports series)
    1. Netball
    I. Title   II. Series
    796.32   GV887

ISBN 0 7134 4799 0

Contents

THE AUTHOR

Sue Campbell is Deputy Director of the National Coaching Foundation.

Having trained as a physical education teacher at Bedford College of Physical Education she subsequently gained a Diploma in Adult and Community Education and a Master of Education Degree at Leicester University.

She is an experienced teacher and held lecturing posts at the Universities of Leicester and Loughborough before working for The Sports Council as regional officer for the East Midlands.

Sue Campbell is a former English Schools athletics international and an England netball player. She was Team Coach to the British Universities Netball and Athletics teams for 1973 to 1979; and continues as a panel coach and umpire for netball and coach to the East Midlands Netball team.

The author (left) in action

ACKNOWLEDGMENT

Special thanks are due to Eileen Langsley of Supersport for her excellent photographs; to George W Dilks for the diagrams and to Mrs Jean Vorderman who somehow managed to read my handwriting and produce the typescript.
Leeds 1985   SC

Introduction

Netball is a fast, exciting game which can be played by people of all ages and abilities. The game is played indoors and outdoors on a hard surface – asphalt, tartan or wood. The court is divided into thirds and each of the seven players on a team has a specific position. Players are restricted to certain areas of the court, they may not travel with the ball and they may not hold the ball for more than three seconds. This creates a rapid passing game which involves all team members working together to move the ball from one end of the court to the other in order to score a goal. Only two of the players on each team may shoot at goal and obstruction and contact are not permitted. The game is controlled by two umpires who ensure fair play.

Netball is popular in school and is played internationally by 31 countries. Every four years netball nations of the world come together to take part in a World Tournament, the most recent of which was in 1987 in Scotland where New Zealand became the World Champions. Many sports have undergone dramatic changes throughout the last century and netball has been no exception. The 'amateur' approach to sport – simply turning up for matches once a week – has been replaced by a more 'professional' approach to training and match play. This does not mean that any of the enjoyment has gone out of the game but it does mean that to reach the top in netball young aspiring players face an exciting challenge and a lot of hard work!

1 The Game

1　How it all began

Games similar to netball were played by the Greeks and Romans in ancient times. Phaimida (Greek) included two of the most important skills found in netball – controlled footwork and skilful ball handling. Trugon (Roman) involved three players in a precise and fast ball handling game. It is also believed that the Aztecs played a game which in its basic concept could be compared to basketball and netball.

The 'modern' game is actually a direct descendant of American basketball. An American visiting Madame Osterberg's College of Physical Training in North London in 1895 showed the students indoor basketball. Like all good teachers he improvised because there were no lines, no circles and no boundaries. The goals were in fact waste-paper baskets hung on the walls at each end of the hall. Later, in 1899, when Madame Osterberg's College had moved from Hampstead to Dartford, another American visitor updated the students on developments in her own country by introducing rings and a larger ball and dividing the court into three areas.

Despite the Victorian attitude to women which deemed any physical activity as degrading and unfeminine, netball developed quite rapidly. This was largely due to the Ling Association which was founded in 1899 by past women students of physical training colleges. By 1901 they had published an official set of rules for netball. Physical training colleges adopted netball as one of their major games for women and consequently it spread rapidly through girls' schools especially in the cities and towns where space was limited. Young women leaving colleges and schools naturally wanted to continue playing and became founder members of clubs throughout the country.

In the 1920s the growth of the suffragette movement helped to enlighten people about the needs of women, especially in the political and professional spheres. It also drew attention to women's rights to take part in physical activities, to be fit and to compete in sports.

1　Netball is a fast and exciting game

The game continued to grow in popularity and the first home international matches took place in 1949 with a triangular fixture between England, Scotland and Wales. However, it was not until 1956 that an overseas team – Australia – visited England and an England team toured abroad in South Africa. It became increasingly obvious that an International Federation needed to be formed to co-ordinate development and standardise the rules throughout the world. A conference was arranged in Ceylon in 1960 and the International Federation of Women's Basketball and Netball Associations was born. The First World Tournament took place three years later at Chelsea College of Physical Education in Eastbourne, Sussex, with eleven countries taking part. Very few spectators were present to witness Australia emerge as the first World Champions. This led an official of the All England Netball Association to say: 'To get the right publicity and the right status desired, the game must emerge from the school playground.'

Unfortunately even today, many people have never seen the game outside the school gates and have never witnessed the thrills and excitement of an International match. The game has an important place inside and outside 'the school playground'. There are currently 3,200 clubs in England and over 42,000 affiliated individuals – predominantly adult women.

2 The court

(i) The ideal court is 30.5 m (100 ft) by 15.25 m (50 ft). The goal circle has a radius of 4.9 m (16 ft) while the centre circle is 0.4 m (3 ft) in diameter.

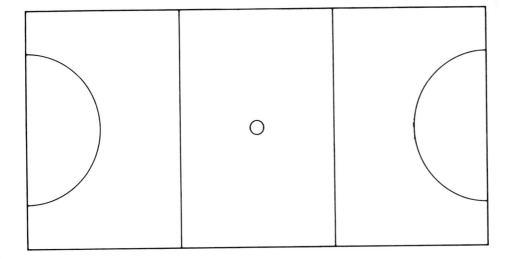

2 *Obvious enjoyment is shown by the players*

(ii) The minimum height of an indoor facility should be 7.6 m (26 ft) with no hanging lights or other projections.

(iii) The surrounding area of the court should have an extra 0.9 m (3 ft) to 1.8 m (6 ft) to provide space for the umpires and officials.

(iv) All court lines (boundaries, thirds and circles) should be 50 mm (2 in.) wide.

The above measurements are ideal. However, if the facilities available are small, the size of the court may be reduced proportionately.

≡ 2 Techniques and Skills ≡

1 Foot control *(Figure 3)*

It is essential for all players to 'know their feet'. Many of the basic techniques of the game are dependent on close control of footwork. Most players focus initially on simply avoiding travelling when in possession of the ball. This is, of course, important because an inability to do this leads to an infringement of the footwork rule (see AENA *Official Netball Rules*, page 23). Advanced players can land efficiently on either foot and make rapid adjustment to regain balance or get into a better position. Beginners usually find it easier to learn a right-footed landing if they are right handed and *vice versa*.

As players become more experienced they develop an ability to make good use of their feet to enable them to execute successfully other skills – throwing, shooting, attacking and defending. 'Alert' feet can be a great asset to any player.

2 Handling the ball *(Figure 4)*

A 'safe pair of hands' is very important and players need to develop a good hand-eye-ball co-ordination. Both beginners and experienced players should take every opportunity to play with the ball in a wide variety of situations. These situations need not be formal netball ones but should allow players to gain experience in manipulating a ball in a number of 'game-like' situations.

(a) Receiving the ball (Figure 5)

In the early stages of learning a player should try to catch the ball with two hands. If she has to take the ball in one hand, she should aim to get the second hand on to the ball as quickly as possible.

Every player should be encouraged to reach out for the ball and 'snatch it' out of the air pulling it in towards their body. Correct timing is essential if this action is to be successful and the player must time not only the extension towards the ball, but also the relaxation of the fingers and the recoil of the arms. The use of hands is obviously important in gaining possession. They should be firm but not stiff and the fingers need to develop a 'sensitivity' for the ball.

A beginner will have to keep her eyes on the ball throughout its flight but

3   Foot control

4 A 'safe pair of hands'

more experienced players will be able to turn their visual attention to the positioning of other players so that they can distribute the ball successfully once it is in their possession.

The ball is usually received in the space ahead and/or above the direction in which the player is moving. This can be difficult for the novice particularly when the thrower may also be having problems judging the correct space and time to place the ball.

(b) Distributing the ball (Figure 6)

Skilful passing involves sending the ball to the right player, in the right space at the right time. In netball the thrower is often faced with an opponent (0.9 m – 3 ft away) defending the pass. This means not only has she to develop good throwing techniques but also she must learn to disguise her true intentions. Flexibility and adaptability are the important qualities shown by good players. It is strength allied to balance and correct timing which will achieve a high level of skill.

A well executed throw is more likely to happen when:
1. The foot corresponding to the throwing hand is to the rear.
2. The feet are shoulder width apart – note that the width of the base will vary according to the height and strength of the player.
3. The feet are pointing in the direction of the throw – careless or sloppy footwork will affect the accuracy of any pass.
4. The preparation for the throw is quick and does not 'give away' the thrower's intention to her opponent.
5. The weight of the body is transferred from the back foot to the front foot before the ball is released.
6. After the ball is released the arms and hands extend in the direction of the pass.

There is a variety of passes used in the game but the throwing techniques are no good in isolation. Players only become skilful when they learn the correct place and time to use the techniques in the game.

The chest pass is normally thrown from chest height and is caught by the receiver between waist and shoulder height. It is usually a direct, hard pass used to move the ball quickly over short or medium distances (depending on the strength of the player's arms and wrists). It is a two-handed pass and the fingers are spread behind the ball with the thumbs pointing towards

6   *Good throwing technique disguising true intentions*

7   *One-handed shoulder pass*

each other. To prepare for the throw the player draws the ball back slightly and 'cocks' the wrists. The elbows are then extended and the wrists and fingers are rapidly flexed or snapped to apply force to the ball. At the same time the weight of the body is moved into the throw by transferring the weight of the body in the direction of the throw.

The one-handed shoulder pass (figure 7) – the ball is released at or slightly above head height. It is a strong direct pass often used to send the ball quickly over long distances. The fingers are spread and pointing upwards, the palm cupped and the thumb placed laterally to provide support for the ball. To prepare for the throw, the player raises the ball above and to the rear of the right shoulder (right handed) and rotates the hips and shoulders to the side. As the player 'unwinds', the elbow, wrist and fingers extend in the direction of the throw. The transfer of weight from the back foot (right foot for right handed player) to the front foot gives the throw added power.

The bounce pass is a very useful pass in a crowded area or when faced with tall defenders. It may be released and caught at a variety of heights and often takes longer to arrive at its destination than an airborne pass. This pass may be made with one or two hands and the preparation will vary accordingly (see the chest pass and the one-handed shoulder pass). The secret of a successful bounce pass is where it bounces. The ball needs to strike the floor approximately two-thirds of the way between sender and receiver or just behind the feet of a tight marking defender. It should be thrown with equal force to the two previous passes and should be 'driven' towards the receiver by transferring the weight into the pass and extending the arm and fingers in the direction of the pass. Weak passes will happen if players 'pat' the ball into the ground rather than 'skim' the ball off the surface to the receiver.

The overhead pass is usually thrown from directly above the head but the exact position will depend on the angle of release required. This pass may be fast and direct or for tactical reasons it may be lifted and lobbed over the heads of the defence. The fingers are spread pointing upwards and the thumbs directed towards each other. As the player prepares to throw she flexes her elbows and keeps them pointed outwards. The ball is propelled forward by extending the elbows but the main force comes from the wrists and fingers. The ball is released in front of the head and any additional force needed may come by moving the body weight into the throw.

The underarm pass is a one-handed pass used to send the ball under the arms of the player defending the ball. It needs to be played carefully and not simply 'slung' to a team-mate. This pass is executed in the same way as the other one-handed passes and can add variety to the attacking play.

It must be re-emphasised that being able to perform the various techniques is no use unless the players know when and where to use the passes effectively.

(c)   Shooting (figure 8)
Being able to score goals is crucial. It may be true that some players have a 'natural' talent for goal-scoring but every player should be given the opportunity to practise and develop shooting techniques. Players can be taught the basic principles from which to work but as with most skills individuals will develop their own style. There is no right or wrong way, success is getting the ball past the defence and into the net.

The following guidelines will help to give a good foundation on which to build:

Feet – in contrast to the throwing action, a shooter stands with the same foot forward as her shooting hand. The width of her feet tends to be narrow but it must be wide enough to give her good balance.

Hands – players may hold the ball in one or two hands. When two hands are used the dominant hand (right hand for right handed player and vice versa) launches the ball towards its target and the other hand stabilizes the ball. The wrist of the dominant hand is cocked and the ball supported on the base of the fingers. The fingers are well-spread on the rear of the ball. The elbow is directly under the hand and the forearm is held straight on the vertical plane.

Eyes – the eyes should focus on the part of the ring furthest from the shooter.

Action – the shooter commences action with a slight flexion of the knees. She then pushes up, giving the necessary power to help propel the ball towards the ring. The ball is projected away high, with a full extension of the arm and a wrist-snap. The fingers relax as the ball is released and follow-through in a downward direction. The ball is usually delivered with back-spin and it should have sufficient height to evade the defence and arrive over the ring. The perfect shot will drop directly through the ring. Shooters should always be encouraged to follow up their shot but they must avoid making contact with the defence.

It is possible to shoot while moving but this requires good footwork and a

21

mastery of the basic shooting technique. Where players are shooting on the move, they need to adjust their arm action to avoid overshooting or undershooting the target. It is also an advantage for shooters to be able to step forward (for example, at a penalty) – the step forward must be within the footwork rule – or step backwards (to gain distance from a defender) in a controlled manner as they shoot for goal.

Shooting is partly a question of confidence and players need to practise taking shots from every part of the circle. Good shooters are able to concentrate on the task in hand and cope with any pressure placed on them. It is difficult to 'keep cool' when the result of the match can depend on their final effort, but with sufficient training they can be helped to withstand almost anything.

3 Attack

There are a number of ways of 'losing' an opponent and 'finding space'. However, it is important that every player understands some basic principles to help her determine what, where and when to perform the various skills in her repertoire.

First of all, *she must know herself.* Every player develops a 'favourite' move – something she can do with ease and execute effectively. This can be a strength but it may also become a weakness. It is vital for attackers to be adaptable and have several different answers to any questions posed by the defence.

Players must also know their own physical limitations so that they can work to make the most of their attributes and not attempt the impossible. This does not mean that they cannot increase their capacities by training but it helps them to set realistic targets.

Timing is a vital part of an attacker's play and learning 'when to go' is gained through practice and experience. Most beginners make the mistake of setting off too early and getting trapped by the defender. Experienced players learn to wait patiently and then make one very decisive move.

Secondly, a player must quickly *assess her opponent.* It is important to find her weaknesses and avoid 'playing into her hands'. Which dodge does she use most frequently? Which hand does she prefer to catch the ball with? Knowing an opponent can help a player dominate and control the game for herself.

There are two main ways of losing defenders – change of speed and change of direction.

(a) *Sprint dodges* may be used during the game to shake off an opponent. If this is to be effective, it needs to be well timed and performed decisively – any 'dithering' will result in confusion and failure. *A straight SPRINT* is often used at the centre pass when the attacker simply sprints forward to receive the centre pass after the whistle has been blown. During play when both the attacker and the defender are in motion, a sudden change of speed can be an effective way of gaining an advantage.

Another ploy which may be used is to sprint rapidly in a given direction, completely stop or decelerate to a jog and then sprint again into a free space *SPRINT-STOP-SPRINT*. This ploy is often used when an attacker finds that her defender is as quick as she is across the court. The deceleration or stop catches the defender unawares, she checks her forward movement, and is then left behind as the attacker sprints off again. Similarly, a sudden *change of direction* can surprise and outwit the opposition: *SPRINT-CHANGE DIRECTION-SPRINT (Figure 9)*. The success of this manoeuvre depends on the attacker's agility, good footwork and decisiveness.

(b) *Feint dodges* may also be used by a player when she has a restricted area in which to move, and is closely marked. In this situation she has neither the time nor space to use a sprint, and may find the feint dodge her best method of losing an opponent. She feints to move in one direction – committing the defender – and then moves off in the opposite direction. The success of this dodge largely depends on the efficiency of the decoy movement. It must be large enough to 'fool the defender' but small enough not to throw the attacker off balance and waste time.

Sometimes it is necessary for the attacker to do two decoy movements – *a double feint dodge* – in order to lose her opponent. these ploys may be used in sideways direction or a forward-backward direction. To accomplish any of these dodges successfully, players need to have good footwork control, move quickly and above all be decisive.

(c) *Developing attacking skills*   When players have mastered the various techniques required to perform the different attacking ploys, then they must begin to develop an awareness of when and where to use them within the game. Choosing the most appropriate method of attack will depend on many factors but players should be continuously *thinking* as well as moving.

The timing of the move is based on judging when the thrower is going to release the ball. This will vary enormously and it is only by exposing players

9   *Sprint dodge – change of direction*   **25**

10   Team attack

11   Defence and attack

to a variety of situations that they are able to develop their own decision-making processes. (Figure 10.)

Players need to develop a large repertoire of *techniques* so that they can produce a variety of responses to any situation. Keeping defenders guessing and surprising them with unexpected changes of tactics is a sure way to gain the upper hand.

This is made easier if the attacker can move equally well to both sides of the body and catch with either hand. It is important for players to be able to take-off from either foot and reach out to catch the ball at full stretch all around the body.

Another quality displayed by many good players is *anticipation*. This can be developed by learning to 'read' the game and watching players 'off the ball'. Too many players concentrate only on the player with the ball which restricts their vision and prevents them from seeing all the possibilities. Anticipation requires an understanding of the whole game and a knowledge of the part each person plays in the total team pattern. In the early stages of learning the game, every girl should be given experience in all the positions so that she can get a 'feel' for the part each team member will play in successfully, moving the ball up the court. Watching the players from whom the pass will be received, assessing the space that is available and knowing where other attackers are situated, all help to improve anticipation.

Linked very closely with this is the ability to *'move off the ball'*. This simply means keeping involved in the game *all* the time – not resting when the ball is at the other end or relaxing after making a successful pass. It means watching carefully, adjusting position constantly and preparing to make the best use of the space available. In this way players can be sure that they are ready to react to any situation and respond effectively.

4 Defence

There are several ways of marking an attacker but the basic requirements are the same. First of all, the player's attitude is fundamentally important to her success as a defender! Concentration is vital and can be improved by devoting time and effort to its achievement. The defender must try to take the initiative and 'call the tune' rather than simply respond to the attacker's moves. She must always be mentally involved in the game. Involvement in the game (no matter where the ball is situated) is very important, and the defensive player must continuously alter her positioning according to the immediate situation.

Persistence is also required to keep working at gaining possession. The defender must try to prevent the attacker successfully receiving the ball; if

12   Careful marking of player from behind

13 *Marking player by standing at right angles*

she fails she immediately tries to stop the attacker making a successful pass, if she fails she must go back to marking the player. This ability to transfer quickly from defending a player to defending the ball needs to be developed physically *and* mentally.

Resilience is another quality she will need as she will have as many (if not more) failures as 'successes' in each game. It is important for her to have a realistic attitude and to recognise that she can only do her own job to the best of her ability and cannot be 'held responsible' for every goal scored by the opposition.

(a) Marking an opponent (first phase defence) – is an essential technique for all players – attackers as well as defenders. Determination is a crucial factor in staying close enough to the opponent to intercept the pass or force an error by the thrower. With beginners the biggest problem is having to split their attention between the ball and their opponent without losing sight of one or the other or (even worse) both! Initially the best method to teach is marking from in front of the opponent. To do this effectively, the defender should take up a position in front of the attacker covering half or three-quarters of her opponent's body with her own and *remaining facing the ball*. The base (feet) should be narrow, the body upright and the arms held with elbows bent so that hands are chest high – ready to reach out and snatch the ball. Any movement should be with small quick steps so that the body weight is kept over the base thus allowing the defender to change speed and/or direction rapidly.

Beginners initially need to watch their opponent very carefully, only turning to look for the ball at the last possible moment. As players become more skilful, they learn to split their attention between the opponent and the ball. If the attacker moves out of vision behind the defender, she must turn her head quickly so that she can keep her opponent almost continuously in view. (*Figure 11*).

It is possible to mark a player from behind but this requires great agility and speed to manoeuvre around the attacker without causing 'contact'. (*Figure 12*.) The advantage is that the marker can watch her opponent *and* see the ball coming down the court. This may enable her to anticipate the pass to her opponent and to move out to successfully intercept. On the other hand there is a tendency for the defender to make contact with her arms or body as she attempts to reach the ball.

A compromise between marking in front and marking from behind is to stand at right angles to the opponent. (*Figure 13*.) This style is adopted by many defenders, particularly in the shooting circle. The defender takes up a position at the side of the attacker, either facing her, or with her back towards her, forming a right angle between her own body and the body of her opponent. Wherever possible she positions herself so that she can see both the attacker and the ball. It is also advantageous if she can stand between the ball and her opponent, forcing the thrower into a long overhead pass.

Every defender should experiment with all three types of stance to determine their own most successful method. It is also esential that defenders are versatile and can vary their tactics (ie defending positions) to 'keep the attacker guessing'.

(b) *Defending the pass* – second phase defence (*Figure 14*) – once the attacker has gained posession of the ball, the defender's attention switches from the player to the ball. She must stand 0.9 m (3 ft) away from the attacker's landing foot or feet, and attempt to prevent her opponent making a successful pass. There are two ways she can achieve this and both require practice. She may choose to jump to intercept the pass but if she fails her opponent may speed away before she lands again. The other method is simply to remain with both feet on the ground and use her full reach to guard the ball. In either case the defender should make sure that her arms are stretched and her hands are covering the ball, not simply waving aimlessly in the air. Defenders will have to decide which method to use based on what they learn about their opponent in the first few minutes of the game. It is always useful to adopt different styles so that the thrower is not sure what to expect.

(c) *Defending the shot (Figure 15)* – obviously this is a technique used only by goal keepers and goal defences during the game, but it is useful to allow everyone the opportunity to experience it at some time. The aim of the action is to prevent a goal being scored and to regain possession of the ball. The defender may achieve this by deflecting or intercepting the shot or causing the shooter to alter her natural technique to a less successful one.

As with defending the pass, the shooter may jump to intercept or keep in contact with the ground and simply use her reach to cause problems for the shooter. The defender needs to practice both methods and to adopt the appropriate one. The decision about which one to use will be based on the height of the opponent in relation to her own (smaller or taller) and the shooter's style (low or high action). For example, a tall goal keeper marking a much smaller goal shooter or one who has a low shooting action, may be

14 Defending the pass

15 Defending the shot

16 Rebounds from net

able to disrupt her action by simply stretching out and covering the ball with her hands. Whereas if the shooter is taller or has a high shooting action, the goal keeper may need to jump to achieve any success.

Once the ball has left the shooter's hand(s), the defender still has to work to get the ball for her own team. Fortunately, she has a team mate with whom she can work and they must know clearly what is going to happen following the release of the ball by the shooter. If the shot for goal is unsuccessful, then between them the defenders *must* try to ensure that the shooters are not given a second chance. (*Figure 16.*) As with all defending skills, the job is never done until the final whistle blows!

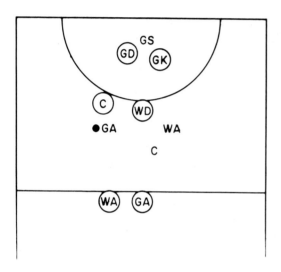

Zone defence in the opposing goal third

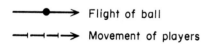

Flight of ball

Movement of players

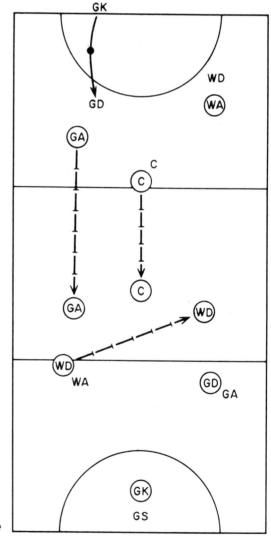

A mid-court zone defence

(d) Developing defending skills – the most important thing is to prevent the opposition from 'dictating' the tactics. It is important that players are armed with several methods of disrupting attacking play and are capable of adapting to whatever situation they find themselves in during the game. It is important as a team to know their own strengths and weaknesses as well as those of the opponents. Players have to realise that no matter how successfully they have 'rehearsed' certain tactics, they are not necessarily going to work against every team they meet. It is also crucial that the team can operate independently of the coach. They must *think* as they play – it is no good waiting until half-time to change an unsuccessful tactic – the game may already be lost.

The most commonly used form of defence is tight 'man-to-man' marking. The nature of the game dictates that this is usually the most effective method of disrupting an attack. Each player has responsibility for marking one member of the opposite team. There are occasions when defenders may find it beneficial to *'switch'* players but this requires good understanding and close co-operation between team members.

The other possible style of team defence is to adopt a zone defence. In zoning each defender marks an area of the court rather than a particular player. The problem for most players when introduced to zoning for the first time is that they are conditioned to following an opponent and get 'drawn out' of the zone leaving a gap which the attacking team can exploit. There is no doubt that a well co-ordinated team zone can be most effective, particularly if it can be used as an alternative to a good man-to-man system.

3 Set Plays

1 Centre pass

The centre pass is very important and should be practised frequently. Playfrom a centre pass ought to result in a goal but even at the highest level errors occur. It is necessary for each team to have a clear strategy worked out and every player should know her own individual job. As with all planned tactics, it is also essential that players are prepared and ready to respond to what might be a totally unexpected situation. (*Figure 17.*) A successful centre pass does not merely consist of the first pass but also the subsequent pattern of play into the circle where a goal is scored.

(a)   Attacking team play
There are several ways of indicating which player will take the first pass.

Signs or signals are used by some teams. One player on the team (usually the centre of goal keeper) gives a previously determined signal to indicate who is to make the first move. The main problem with this method is that any lapse of memory on the part of signaller or team can result in chaos.

Another method used is a *rota system* where a set order is adhered to in sequence. The order may be remembered by using a particular word. Each letter in the word indicates which player is to move for the centre pass. For example APPLE: A = Goal Attack, P = Wing Attack, P = Wing Attack, L = Goal Defence, and E = Wing Defence. The centre starts at the beginning of the word and keeps repeating it through. Young players often enjoy making up a new code word and this system works well as long as the players do not lose track of the word. More experienced players may simply work to a set order of passes and require no cues or words to help them remember which player is to move for the pass.

Another even simpler method is for one player (most often the wing attack) to receive the centre pass constantly. If she can do this successfully, there may be no need to develop more complex systems. It is important to remember that the *SIMPLE way is always best*.

The Centre in possession of the ball should be wholly inside the centre circle. The opposing Centre is in the centre third and free to move. The attacking Centre should adopt a symmetrical base as close to the edge of the circle as possible. From this position she can step in any direction and

17   WA prepares to move out for centre pass

move her feet to allow efficient distribution of the ball. The starting positions of the other players will largely be determined by what is to follow. The player moving for the first pass must try to ensure that she has a starting position which will allow her to move out rapidly for the pass.

The second pass is equally important. Who will receive the second pass and where it is received will be dictated by where the first pass is caught. The team may devise a pattern of passes from the centre which involve a

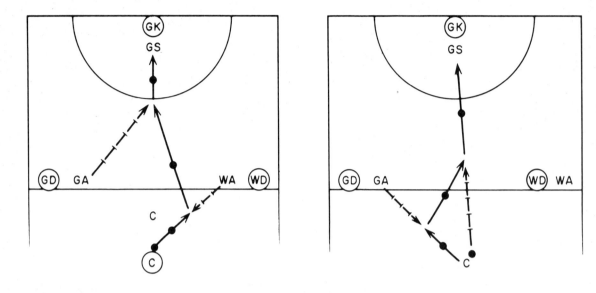

Attacking tactics at the centre pass

number of players working to a set plan. This can be useful but it is important to have flexible plan which can be easily adapted when the unexpected happens.

(b) Defending team play (Figure 18)
The defending centre needs to assess the situation and determine her action according to the opposition's tactics. She may adopt a tight man-to-man defence covering the pass of her opponent and try to make an accurate pass difficult. If she fails she will immediately mark her opponent and attempt to prevent or delay her next contribution to the attacking play. As the game progresses it may be come clear that one of the attacking players is repeatedly and successfully receiving the first pass. In this situation the defending centre may choose to drop back away from her own opponent to double-defend the dangerous attacker. A third option she has is to mark the attacking area of the centre court between wing attack and goal attack. This can prevent these players moving into the central area of the court to receive the centre pass and force them wide to the edges of the court.

18 Intercepting the pass

The other defending players should try to break down the attacking play as early as possible. Before the whistle is blown, players usually 'jostle' for position and it is at this time that the defender must try to take the initiative. She can do this by giving her opponent a limited choice of space and possibly making her take the pass on her weaker side. (*Figure 19.*) If the centre pass has been well practised, the defender may have no chance of intercepting the first pass. By lunging to intercept the pass, she can in fact be placing herself at a disadvantage. She must then decide whether to continue with this action or whether to modify it so that she is in a position to cover the pass made by her opponent and then make the next attacking move more difficult.

2 Side and goal line throw-in

When the ball goes out of courts, the rules state that it must be put into play by any member of the opposing team allowed in that area. This means that a team often has a choice about who takes the throw-in. Several factors should influence their decision. The first consideration is the position on court where the throw-in is to be taken and the throwing capabilities of the various team members. Secondly, it will be necessary to assess the strengths and weaknesses of the opposition and the space available on the court.

As with the centre pass, it is possible to work out set patterns of play but this rigid approach may prove to be too easily read by the opposition. One simple basic plan is for players to 'screen' space. In this play the player nearest the thrower remains in the space until the umpire calls 'play'. She then moves out and allows the next nearest player to move into the space she has vacated to receive the pass. This ensure that the throw-in will have a short distance to travel and should avoid too much indecision amongst the attacking team.

3 Penalties

With the exception of the throw-up, penalties are awarded to a team not to a particular player. This means that any member of the 'offended' team can take the penalty pass or shot. Once a penalty has been awarded, the offender must remain next to the penalty-taker until the pass or shot has been taken. To take full advantage of this, the attacking team members must react quickly and decisively. A rapid pass may catch the opposition defence out of position and capitalise on their error. In other situations it will be beneficial for the thrower to take the pass less rapidly allowing her team mates to re-form and organise their attack. In both cases it is important that the team members know who is to take the pass and what she will do, so that they can react accordingly.

If a defender offends in the shooting circle, the attacker may choose to pass or shoot. An understanding between the two shooters is essential in these circumstances. They may agree that the better shooter will take all the penalties or that they will feign to shoot and then pass if the penalty is on the edge of the circle. Whatever they decide teamwork, speed and an element of surprise are essential.

4   The toss up (*Figure 20*)

This is given when two players simultaneously gain possession of the ball or break a rule. The umpire stops the game and the two players stand 0.9 m (3 ft) apart each facing her own goal. As with shooting, players will develop their own way of achieving success but there are certain general guidelines which are helpful particularly for inexperienced players.

The stance may vary but most players adopt a narrow base with one foot in front of the other. This gives greater stability and balance. The arms must be in line with the sides of the body and should be held with a degree of tension. They should be neither rigid nor relaxed, as this would prevent them being moved rapidly. Hands should be open with fingers slightly spread so that the ball could be 'snatched' out of the air. The player's eyes need to focus on the point where the ball rests on the umpire's hand, as this is where the first movement will occur.

If she is successful the player should try to take the ball away from the direction of the opponent and prepare to make a pass or shot. If she fails she should immediately defend the pass or shot.

The other players need to be aware of the space available to them if their team mate gains possession of the ball and equally aware of the possible movements of their opponents should she not win the throw up.

Throw ups should be practised in every area of the court involving each team member. This will help players react quickly and effectively in any situation.

20 *The throw up*

4 Ball Handling Practice Sessions

The construction of any practice session will vary according to the age and experience of the players.

1 Younger/Less experienced group

(a) Warm up
The basic warm up (as described in Chapter 5) should be followed by simple skills or activities learnt in previous sessions (footwork, ball handling).

(b) Skill phase
This is where players learn a new skill or develop work which they started previously. At the very early stages it will be necessary to give individuals as much experience of handling the ball as possible – *ball familiarisation*. Players should develop sensitivity and learn to control the ball. Initially each player will need to work on this alone without any outside distractions. Once players have begun to master these skills, they can begin to work with a partner – *co-operative phase*. Finally, this has to be put into the competitive situation and placed under pressure.

Players should not try to cover too much in one session. Two or three different ways of practising the same skill may be devised. It is important to build slowly – brick by brick – skill by skill.

Even at this stage players must be encouraged to think for themselves and not merely 'perform to order'.

(c) Game phase
At the early stages of skill development this should not be a full sided (7 vs 7) game. There are many small sided games which relate to netball. Players may even be able to devise their own! It is the concepts which need to be understood initially before further complications are added! For example, players need to develop an awareness of others; how to use space; how to time their moves; what is meant by *defending* and *attacking*. All this can be learnt in small sided games.

A game of 3 vs 3 in one third of the court can give players ample opportunity of handling the ball and not be over complicated. Every time the *attacking* team has seven consecutive passes they score a goal. The ball is then given to the *opposition* and they attempt to do the same. If the ball is *intercepted* by the *defending* team then they can *keep possession* and try to score a goal. If the ball goes *out of court* or a player goes *offside*, then the *free pass* is given to the opposition. Short *matches* can be played with half-time and an opportunity to discuss *team tactics*. All these concepts need to be learnt and understood in a practical situation.

2   Older/More experienced players

(a) Warm Up
As well as the basic warm up (see Chapter 5) it may include a short game or something from the previous match/session which needs practice.

(b) Skill phase
This may be approached in two ways. Once the teacher/coach has helped the players to identify specific areas needing improvement, then these may be worked on either outside the game as a series of practices or inside the game by using 'action replay' techniques. In some instances it will be necessary to use both. Practices should be *mentally* and physically challenging and always related to the 'real' game situation. Techniques are no good in isolation: they need to be used at the right place, at the right time in order to have the right result.

(c) Game phase
This may be in the form of a conditioned game in which certain additional rules are introduced to ensure that new skills are used in the game. It should also include at this level some tactical or strategical planning. It is often possible to separate the attackers from the defenders to work on ploys, eg attacking play from the centre pass or working the ball out of defence from a back-line throw in. Each player should know her own role and be working as one unit in a team of seven.

EXAMPLES
There are many different practices and players should be encouraged to make up their own. Overleaf is one example of working in 2s, 3s, 4s, 5s, 6s and 7s. Any skill may be learnt using any of these practices.

Key to diagrams

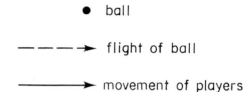

● ball

- - - ➤ flight of ball

──────➤ movement of players

In 2s

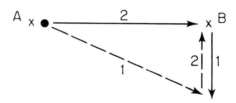

A starts with the ball
B moves to left or right and indicates
A throws the ball to B
As soon as B is balanced A moves off to receive her pass and so on.

In 3s

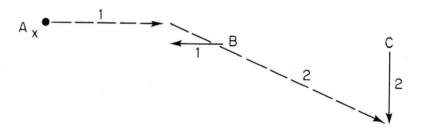

A starts with the ball
B runs forward
A passes the ball high so that B jumps and turns in the air as she catches the
    ball
B lands, balances
C moves to left or right and receives the ball from B.

48

In 4s

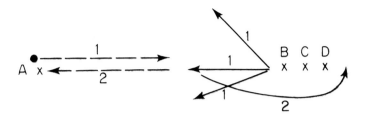

A starts with the ball
B moves forward *in any direction* to receive the ball from A
B returns the ball to A and then runs to join the back of the queue
C then moves forward to receive a pass from A and so on.

In 5s

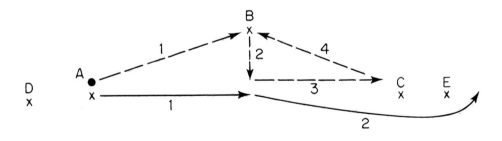

A starts with the ball
A throws to B and moves forward to receive a return pass from B
A then runs behind D
C passes the ball to B and moves forward to receive the return pass
C catches the ball from B and immediately throws to D and so on.

In 6s

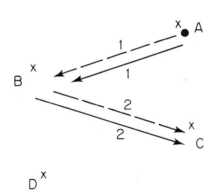

B stands in the middle of a circle of players

A starts with the ball

A throws to B who is standing in the centre of the circle

B catches the ball and immediately throws to C

B moves out of the centre of the circle towards C as A runs into the centre of the circle to receive the ball from C

A then passes to D and moves out of the centre as C moves in to receive the pass from D and so on.

In 7s Half court game

A team can practice using half the court with the defence playing against their own attack

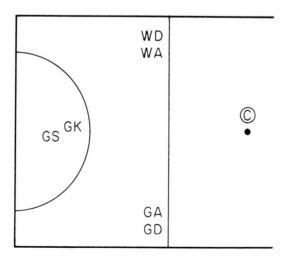

Play may commence with a centre pass or it can begin with a throw in from the back line by the defence This is often a useful way of practising team tactics as well as specific skills.

5 Preparing to Play

1 Warm up and cool down

Warm up – Before training or matches it is essential to prepare both the body and mind for action. There are three main reasons why warm up is essential:
- It assists the body's organs – heart and lungs – to cope with sudden demands placed on it by intensive exercise.
- It may help to protect against injury.
- It will give players an opportunity to focus on the job in hand and get off to a better start.

The basic warm up consists of three phases.
It begins with some steady jogging to get the whole body warm.
This is followed by stretching exercises. These need to be done slowly and carefully. Rapid, bouncing movements must be avoided and all the muscle groups in the body stretched.
The final stage is to do some dynamic, fast running over short distances (eg shuttle runs) to ensure that each individual is ready for action.

As teams get more experienced they build a routine of ball handling practices to follow this basic warm up before matches. Throughout the warm up each player needs to concentrate and prepare themselves mentally as well as physically.

The diagram overleaf gives an indication of the type of pre-match warm up which will take place before a game. In competitive situations it is vitally important to have the right length of warm up. If a team spends too long doing a vigorous warm up then fatigue may set in and if the warm up is too short it will not prepare the players properly. It is not possible to prescribe the exact length of warm up as this varies according to the age and fitness of the players, but on average 15 minutes is considered to be adequate for most teams.

Cool down – When the training session or match is over it is equally vital for players to cool down. The body's organs are still in top gear and before the engine can be switched off there is a need to reduce speed and calm down. If the players do not cool down they may feel particularly stiff and uncomfortable the next day! Cooling down usually consists of some light steady jogging and a few loosening exercises.

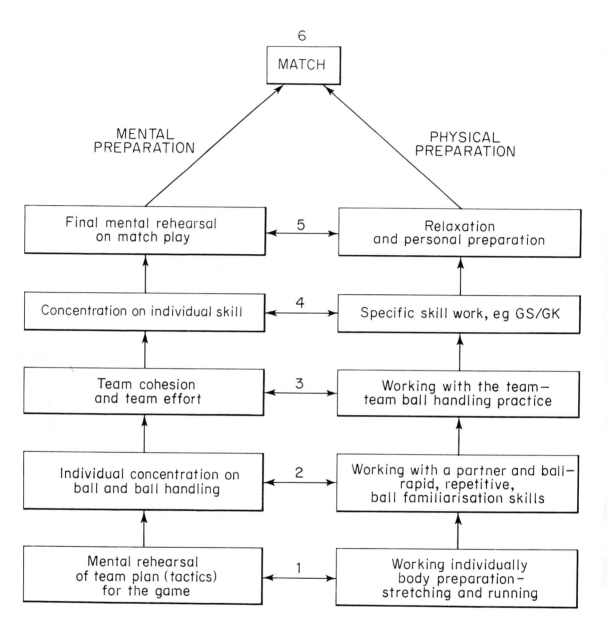

                        6
                     ┌─────────┐
                     │ MATCH │
                     └─────────┘

MENTAL   PHYSICAL
PREPARATION   PREPARATION

Final mental rehearsal on match play	←5→	Relaxation and personal preparation
Concentration on individual skill	←4→	Specific skill work, eg GS/GK
Team cohesion and team effort	←3→	Working with the team— team ball handling practice
Individual concentration on ball and ball handling	←2→	Working with a partner and ball— rapid, repetitive, ball familiarisation skills
Mental rehearsal of team plan (tactics) for the game	←1→	Working individually body preparation— stretching and running

Pre-match warm up ladder

21 *Stamina, speed, strength, suppleness and skill are needed*

2 Fit to play

Every player should have a training programme which consists of ball skills, team practices and body conditioning. If a player neglects any of these aspects, she will not be able to fulfil her potential. For a training process to have any meaning, each player needs to consider what she is required to do in the game and ensure that she prepares accordingly. Stamina, speed, strength, suppleness and skill may all be achieved with the correct training methods. Mental preparation is equally important and players must develop the right approach to training and match play.

(a) Physical conditioning

All netball players should be 'athletes' with different skills and abilities according to their chosen position. It is often easy to neglect fitness because it seems less attractive than playing a game or practising particular techniques. It requires determination, perseverance and the will to succeed. Training takes place all year round and varies in intensity according to the time of year and the level of competition. There are many different ingredients in a good fitness programme and there is no easy way to achieve top-class condition. A general training programme should consist of running (variations of fast and slow pace), circuit training, weight training (for older players 16+), ball handling and team practice. With careful planning, fitness training can be varied and enjoyable as well as rewarding.

(i) **Running** should include long (2-5 miles – 3-8 kilometres) steady runs to build basic stamina and interval running to help condition the body for the type of activity encountered in netball. Running over open country can provide the opportunity to do some fast and slow pace running (fartlek).

Example of fartlek running:
– Easy running 10 minutes
– Half pace 300 m
– Walk 5 minutes
– A series of 50 m sprints interspersed with easy jogging
– Walk until recovered
– Fast pace for as long as possible, then jog gently to finish.

Interval running may be done using a netball court.

EXAMPLE
- Start at A and go through the series shown below without stopping
- Rest for 45 seconds
- Repeat
- Rest for 45 seconds
- Repeat

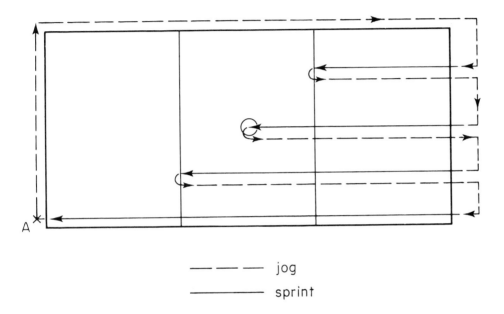

— — — — jog
——————— sprint

(ii) **Circuit training** provides an excellant way of exercising the whole body. It can improve muscular endurance, flexibility and general body conditioning. A typical circuit used by netball players would probably consist of:

Trunk curls Lie on your back with your hands behind your head: bend your knees so that your legs are not straight, keep your feet flat on the ground. Sit up and touch both knees with both elbows.

Astride jumps on a bench   Stand astride a
bench (or other suitable platform)
approximately 30 cm high; jump with both
feet into a standing position on the bench;
then jump back to the original astride position.
Repeat this rhythmically and continuously.

Press ups   Start in the front support position;
bend your arms to lower your chest to the
floor; and return to the front support position.
Keep your body rigid throughout with no
sagging in the lower back, and your arms
shoulder-width apart.

Step ups Step on and off a chair or bench 30 cm high: make sure that your legs and back are perfectly straight when both feet are on the chair.

Salmon snaps Lie on your back with your arms straight above your head. Sit up raising both arms and feet simultaneously to make a 'V' shape. Return to laying flat on the ground.

Squat thrusts Start in the front support position; jump with both feet into the crouch position, jump with both feet back to the front support position. Repeat this rhythmically and continuously.

The number of repetitions of each exercise will vary according to the players involved, but a typical circuit would be:

	Repetitions
Trunk curls	10
Astride jumps on a bench	20
Press ups	8 or max
Step ups	10 each leg leading
Salmon snaps	10
Squat thrusts	8

Players should go all the way through this circuit three times without stopping. They should work at full speed and take the total time. Each player should record her own time and work to improve it.

It is also possible to combine skill and endurance work. This places the skills under pressure which is what usually happens in the game.

(iii) **Skill endurance circuit**
1   20 chest passes against a wall into a marked square.
    Catch the rebound.
2   10 trunk curls
3   20 shoulder passes into a marked target
4   20 astride jumps on a bench
5   20 overhead passes – two hands – into a marked target
6   10 squat thrusts
7   10 shots at goal (only allowed to count those that score!)
8   10 step ups (left leg leading); 10 step ups (right leg leading)
9   20 two handed side passes (use alternate sides)
10 6 shuttle runs

It is important to work for accuracy as well as speed because quality of performance is essential.

(iv) **Weight training**   It is important, and indeed essential, for all speed athletes (which includes netball players) to be strong. For this reason alone netball players should be looking for ways of improving their strength, mobility and endurance through weight training and circuit training. Weight training is however very specialised and should not be done without close supervision. In most cases it is not advisable to begin using weights until players can handle their own body weight and the growth spurt of adolescence is over (15, 16 years of age).

(b) Mental preparation

Simple physical condition alone is no guarantee of success in netball. Players must also have the right mental approach and be encouraged to develop the right decision making mechanism. Learning 'thinking skills' is as vital as learning physical skills. Practices should not take place mindlessly. Players must work their minds as well as their bodies. Being able to 'read the game' can be learnt if individuals are given practices requiring them to think for themselves rather than merely execute 'drills'.

Every team will need to feel that they are making progress so it is important that they are helped to focus on what they are capable of achieving, both in the long term and in the short term. In the long term it may be that the team wish to win the end of season county schools tournament. In the short term it may be that they are simply aiming to improve their play out of defence. Each player should know clearly what they are expected to do and what part they have to play in the teams performance. This will give them confidence and encourage cohesion.

Finally, players should not be afraid to experiment. It is important that they do not become so scared of making mistakes that they never attempt anything new. Every player needs to explore the full range of their talent and recognise that they will make errors. It is by doing this they will learn and develop their own individuality.

(c) Training programmes

(c) Training programmes should help to prepare players in every way – ball handling, team practice, physical conditioning and mental preparation. No one element ought to be neglected. The amount of time spent on each element will vary according to the time of year and what events are on the calendar.

A typical in-season programme may be seen below:

Saturday	Match
Sunday	Run 1 ½/2 – 2-3 kilometres varying speed – fartlek
Monday	Ball handling and circuit training
Tuesday	Team practice (tactics and strategy)
Wednesday	Ball handling and shuttle running
Thursday	Skill – endurance circuit
Friday	Rest day

Pre-season training will contain more body conditioning sessions and skills sessions.

Wherever possible training programmes should be varied and interesting. Players themselves should be involved in working out the schedules and learn to monitor their own progress.

Training diaries – players should try to keep a diary. They ought to record every training session in detail so that they can map their progress and develop the schedule with the help of the coach. The diary should also include matches played with results and comments about individual and team performances. Finally the players should record any injuries incurred and the treatment which followed. This way both the player and the coach can begin to assess what type of programme produces the best results.

3   Pre-match preparation

A good warm up session prior to a match can help pre-match nerves and give players confidence to face the opposition. Players should avoid any intensive training for 24 hours before important games. The body requires this time to refuel its engines otherwise energy stores are depleted and players may 'fade' during the game.

Pre match meals should not be eaten too close to playing. It is preferable to eat three (or at least two) hours before playing. This allows the body to digest the food and use it to provide energy. Some foods are more quickly converted to provide energy than others. Carbohydrates – bread, biscuits, pasta, potatoes – are all good sources of 'instant' fuel. It is difficult to prescribe the ideal pre match meal. Generally players should eat what they enjoy but not over-indulge!

4   Post-match analysis

When games are over it is usually a time of celebration or disappointment. Once the immediate emotions have passed, it is important that every player takes a good look at their performance. They need to assess with the assistance of their teacher or coach where they did well, where they need more practice, and what lessons they have learnt. The next training session should be built around those observations so that they continue to improve. Individual players and the team as a whole should build on their strengths and recognise those areas needing improvement. Every game should present a new challenge, a new opportunity to work on some skill or strategy. No matter how good a player becomes, she can always find room for improvement.

6 The Winning Formula

There is no doubt that winning is more fun than losing, but what do we mean by winning? There is much more to winning than simply defeating the opposition. Every player has a certain level of skill which she should be working to improve whenever she plays. This includes the execution of individual skills and her contribution to the overall team effort. Her own personal targets may be set with the guidance of the teacher or coach so that she has a realistic chance of success. She may simply be asked to improve one particular aspect of her own game (eg throwing) or given a specific job to do within the team. This means that despite defeat for the team she may well have triumphed in her 'own game'.

Developing the right attitude to achieving success is like crossing a river using stepping stones. Players should stand on one bank – their starting point – and take a good look across the river to see the other bank – the finishing point. They can then plan their passage across the river using the stepping stones and assess how long the journey will take. Each stone is another step forward in the right direction. Players may occasionally slip and get their feet wet – this should not worry them – very few people manage to achieve success without some setbacks. Every training session, every match and every season should be carefully planned to help the player reach their potential (the other bank).

Finally, for those who are determined to reach the top there is no substitute for practice and training. A player who wishes to do well and become successful has to be willing to learn and prepared to work hard. No matter how good they become, there is always some part of their game which can be improved.

Further Reading, Videos and Films

Planning a Tournament, by Mary Thomas (AENA)
The Netball Coaching Manual, edited by Heather Crouch, A & C Black, 1984 (available from AENA as well)
Netball Today, Phyl Edwards and Sue Campbell, Lepus Books, 1980, available from A & C Black
Know The Game Netball, available from AENA

AENA publications

Official Netball Rules
Netball Skills
How to Start Netball
Netball Rules for Young Players
Pick-a-Practice Cards
Official Score Sheet Pads
Netball—The official AENA magazine

Hire AENA video tapes

All tapes are VHS

1   *New Zealand* v *England*
    3rd Test match in New Zealand – Edited June 1981
2   *England* v *New Zealand*
    Robinsons Barley Water International Trophy match at Bletchley – September 1979 – Edited
3   *England* v *Scotland*
    Robinsons Barley Water Trophy match at Coventry – November 1980 – Edited
4   *England* v *New Zealand*
    Robin Wools International Netball Trophy at Wembly Arena 1982
5   *World Tournament – Singapore* 1983
    (a) *England* v *Trinidad*
    (b) *England* v *New Zealand*
    (c) *England* v *Australia*
    (d) *New Zealand* v *Australia* (Final match)
6   *England* v *Scotland*
    Sugar International Netball Trophy at Wembley Arena, November 1983

Orders should be placed six weeks prior to date required. Details from AENA.

Films

Aiming for Wembley. Apply to the AENA for details
The World Championship—New Zealand 1975.
Details from Town and Country Productions Limited, 21 Cheyne Row,
London SW3 5HP

Netball shooting badge scheme

Three levels of award are awarded:
    3rd Class (Green badge)
    2nd Class (Blue badge)
    1st Class (Red badge)
    For details contact the AENA

Training videos for sale from AENA

Basic Umpiring
Advanced Umpiring
Basic Coaching Series No 1
Advanced Coaching Series No 2
Under 12 Coaching Series No 3

The Governing Body of the sport

The All England Netball Association (AENA), Francis House, Francis Street,
London SW1, from which address the above mentioned publications and
details of videos and films can be obtained on request.

The National Coaching Foundation

The National Coaching Foundation provides a service for all coaches
whatever their level of experience. The Foundation has a wide variety of
products available including books, videos and courses. In addition, there is
an information and advisory service. For full details contact the NCF at
4 College Close, Beckett Park, Leeds LS6 3QH   Telephone (0532) 744802

Index